No One Visits the Mother of a **Drug Addict**

Nancy R. Chalmers

Copyright © 2017 by Nancy R. Chalmers

No One Visits the Mother of a Drug Addict
by Nancy R. Chalmers

Printed in the United States of America.

ISBN 9781498492737

All rights reserved solely by the author. The author guarantees all contents are original and do not infringe upon the legal rights of any other person or work. No part of this book may be reproduced in any form without the permission of the author. The views expressed in this book are not necessarily those of the publisher.

Unless otherwise indicated, Scripture quotations taken from the Holman Christian Standard Bible (HCSB). Copyright © 1999, 2000, 2002, 2003, 2009 by Holman Bible Publishers. Used by permission. All rights reserved.

Front and Back Cover graphic design by Andrew Chalmers

www.xulonpress.com

Table of Contents

Introduction vii
Dedication ix
Acknowledgements xi
Chapter 1 The Storm 15
Chapter 2 Our Andrew 25
Chapter 3 The Truth shall set you Free 35
Chapter 4 Put the Baby in the Basket 47
Chapter 5 Is this My Son? 55
Chapter 6 Please Send a Big Fish 69
Chapter 7 Punching Holes in the Darkness 79
Chapter 8 Just Let go and Soar 85
Chapter 9 I Stand Amazed 89
Chapter 10 Happy Dance 95
Chapter 11 Reality Check 99
Chapter 12 Praise and Prayer 107
Notes 111
About the Author 113
Reflections- worksheets for a small group study 115

Introduction

I know why this book has taken me more than three years to write. Healing takes time. God's plans have an eternity to develop. I could never have planned anything remotely like this. No matter how much I love my children, I have no power to take rebellion, pain and sorrow and turn it into joy. My story convinces me again:

God's ways are so much higher!

I am sitting in a guest room at the Teen Challenge Lakeside Retreat in Alabama writing this story. Teen Challenge has blessed me with this time alone. The peace and beauty of my lake view is perfect.

This place affords the quiet time I need to pour out the story our family has traveled. The title of this book exposes the anger and disappointment that filled my heart at the beginning of this project. Reliving the past and all its pain is at best difficult. Thankfully, after a few years of healing it is a bit easier.

It is cold, foggy and rainy outside and I am reminded that someone reading this may be brokenhearted and desperate. Please know that I do not have all the answers. This book began as a healing process for me and has developed into an opportunity to share some treasures God has shown me during this storm.

Families everywhere are dealing with these tough issues.

My prayer for hurting families is that my story leads them to find real Hope and Peace.

A reflective study for personal use or small group participants has been added at the end of this book. These are worksheets for your own personal study. The Facilitator's guide for this small group study is available by contacting the author by email. nrc3353@gmail.com

Dedication

For my children and grandchildren:

I love you. I am so proud of you all.
Continue to Follow Jesus,
Just be held!

Acknowledgements

What an adventure in the unknown. I am not a writer. I do enjoy telling stories. This endeavor has challenged me in many ways, but the compelling from God to comfort others kept me going.

My thanks cannot adequately express my feelings to each one that helped me along this journey.

God Bless these loved ones:

First, my husband Louis walked beside me along this road and was the strong support I needed so many times. Every time I wanted to quit, he would encourage me to take one step at a time.

Olivia, my first born, listened to my heartache and struggles and blessed me with her understanding heart.

Melissa, my sweet daughter, would step in to help with the demands of daily life so I could write this book.

Andrew chose to follow Jesus wholeheartedly and that has made this project such a joy. We have had fun learning how our perspectives and memory are not quite the same for some of the details of this story. He has supported my truth-telling so that many families will find comfort and God's healing. It was so fitting that he use his graphic arts training to design the cover of this book.

Lynn Wolford, my friend who tried to visit me at the wrong hospital and joined in the Happy Dance, was the first one to read my early chapters. She gave me heartfelt encouragement to publish my story.

Wendy Cope was responsible for editing the first draft. I knew I could trust her with this story, and receive no judgement, just in case I decided not to publish it. She was aware that I was writing in my voice, yet corrected the grammar, phrasing placement, and punctuation. More importantly, she understood that while I was writing my story, I was reliving the heartache I had experienced.

Andree Aiken became my writing coach after the first draft was written. I have had teachers in my life, but I have never had a coach. What a blessing she was to this project. Her ability to ask the right questions and help me see where God was leading proved invaluable. Keeping on schedule for this project was difficult, but the special time with her kept me accountable.

Reflection study ladies, you know who you are. Each one of you sharpened the focus of each chapter by participating in the first group study. Sharing this time with you and listening to your struggles encouraged me to continue. Your grateful responses were another validation that many need to hear my story.

Finally, Julia Odom, a long time kindred spirit, came to my rescue, using her many years of experience, and edited the final draft.

Chapter 1
The Storm

Michael Jackson died today. I have heard every possible speculation and detail about this event. My son is at death's door again, and I find myself in an ER waiting room unable to avoid the 24 hour news. This time as I wait, I am watching the tragic story of another unfold.

No media to cover the details of my son's tragic choices.

Andrew's world of lies, secrecy, and drugs have brought us to another hospital in our area. They all seem the same: you are greeted by a receptionist and then a law enforcement officer. The wait is very short on the outside and very long on the inside. My heart clings to a small amount of hope that this time we will finally find the right help.

Earlier that same afternoon, Andrew had arrived home with his boss and coworkers for a meeting with his father and me. This caring group of coworkers came to explain why they had to fire Andrew from a job at which he was excelling. His gift of selling "ice to an Eskimo" had benefited their business so their decision was a difficult one. Real courage is doing something that costs you. And that is what they did. Not only did they confront him, they escorted him to the hospital.

This visit is the only time I was accompanied by anyone other than my husband. These friends had all been down a similar road. They did not come to visit with me.... but that is what they did.

Their concern was that Andrew would find help. They were the only ones to fully explain to me the truth about his future. I will never forget what they said: "He needs at least two years of rehab. His drugs of choice are some of the most difficult from which to break free."

Of course, my heart sank.

By this point in time nothing surprised me; it was always easier to believe things were better than they truly were, or swing to the other side where there was no hope. I was on a roller coaster between the two.

As I remember that night, I realize now how alone and lost I felt during all the other times my children had been in the emergency room. Andrew's friends tried to help me understand the gravity of the situation we faced. I will always be thankful for their honest conversation.

Then they sat with me for hours, hoping for the right help to become available.

I knew that many hours were ahead in the ER. The guys had lives to go back to. I had waiting and praying to do, while Andrew was monitored by a full time attendant. Living with a drug addict is a nonstop hurricane, and here again, I found peace and quiet during the short-lived calm of its eye. After 20 hours we were sent home.

No help and no hope. No available beds for our son.

Andrew was out of school, out of work and we were almost out of money.

The storm had just begun to intensify in our home. After six weeks in a halfway house, he had been kicked out. Again, we allowed him to move back in our home. This time we knew no one could help, so we began our strongest efforts to save his life.

We seemed to be out of options.

After 30 years of hard work in engineering, my husband's career came to a sudden halt. The economy went into a recession that stopped almost all transportation engineering projects. We experienced a step by step stripping of all the things on which we could depend. To make ends meet, Louis was doing some work out of our home and decided he would oversee Andrew. His daily interaction with Andrew gave him an up-close understanding of drug addiction.

You have never been "played" until you have a lying, manic, charismatic drug addict for a son. With a great deal of persuasive conversation, Andrew convinced his dad that his only hope for recovery was a methadone clinic.

We had no idea what his decision really meant.

He had truly given up on ever getting free.

I remember that as a child, Andrew would stop breathing occasionally as he slept. It would always send a chill up my spine until he could catch his breath. During these last few years, I would go down to his room and see if he was still alive and breathing. Praying the entire way that he was alive.

I could not begin to fathom the chaos I would come home to in the following weeks. Andrew's frantic search for the next solution kept us all in a spin. Not one word could be believed and yet, we always did. We gave him chance after chance, many times being deceived. Even when we did not allow him to drive, his drug buddies would come pick him up.

One day I came home to my husband walking around in total confusion unable to complete a sentence. I knew we were all going to fall apart if help did not come.

Some days his eyes were a bit clearer and our dear Andrew might show up for a short while. He was getting thinner and his sallow complexion uncovered his lies. His charm could convince us he was clean and working hard on his sobriety. He is so smart. My daughter remembers wondering how someone that was so high on drugs, could be so quick-witted and full of answers.

In the same week, he would come in with his full force mania and completely confuse and torment us. My spoons kept disappearing. Some jewelry and other things were gone. His excuses and alibies began to be ridiculous. My husband often reminded me of how much he insulted our intelligence with the stories he told.

One of Andrews's favorite pastimes was "Doctor shopping". When one psychiatrist would catch onto his drug use, he would find another. Recovery meetings were a great place for Andrew to get info on new doctor options to visit next. He knew every way to describe his "ailments" to get the drugs he wanted. This was a legal form of getting the prescription drugs, therefore less dangerous. I was becoming very suspicious of any doctor visit so when Andrew asked me to take him to a doctor's appointment in the wealthiest part of Atlanta, I agreed.

Anyone in their right mind would not set an appointment in that busy part of town at 4:30 in the afternoon.

I knew what he was doing, but I wanted to really see how this worked. I did not go in the building at the same time as Andrew.

I came into the waiting room alone and sat alone. He was called in to see the doctor. I timed the visit: 22 minutes.

Andrew came out with five new prescriptions. I was amazed and furious. Surprisingly, the doctor stepped out to tell Andrew something, I quickly stepped up to ask him a question. He asked me, "And who are you?" I saw him step back as I said, "His mother."

Andrew had not told him he was on methadone. I asked if combining all these prescriptions with his methadone treatment was a problem. Trying not to look surprised, he assured me they would be fine. I was livid. Hearing about a legal drug pusher is one thing, meeting one is quite a different matter.

Andrew spent the entire 50 minute trip home needling me, begging me, trying to convince and then demanding that we get these prescriptions filled. I would not stop the car. I had to pray for clarity of mind just to drive home.

Louis did go and get the drugs, which was when I made my decision to stop participating in this craziness. My answer became "Ask your Father!" Our relationship was shaken by constant disputes over Andrew's care. I resigned myself to the inevitable war, spoke my mind and then I would go to work. My trip to work was about forty-five minutes.

Thirty minutes of crying and praying and fifteen of repairing my makeup to pretend all was well.

One Monday after spending the weekend in the ER, I was helping a client select between a soft taupe and a pale grey paint color for her walls. The lady became distraught over the choices and how much stress it was causing her. It took everything in me not to smack her. She had no idea I had spent the weekend praying my son would live.

I was one of the hidden walking wounded, feeling totally alone. Now, I know "we" are everywhere.

This is not something you share with all the seemingly whole people around you; especially if you are a Bible study leader in a church where this type of pain can be shameful. We did not want him in jail and now had no insurance for a mental hospital.

I am not sure how we survived. Our personal lives, our marriage, our sanity all stressed to the breaking point. Our energy, financial resources and hope were running dry. All of the years of parenting could not prepare us for this storm.

I felt like the demon sorcerer of addiction had moved into our lives tormenting us nonstop. The rules of common sense and the natural world did not apply. Life was consumed with surviving one crisis after another. The details of those months are so foggy. We took very few pictures. I had no desire to remember any of it.

Few Sunday school classes or small group studies address survival with a drug addict. Our times at AA family meetings were so depressing that it would take days to recover. Their "no cure" attitude about addictions did not line up with our beliefs. I discovered that only an in-depth study of God's Word gave me the answers.

Over 2700 years ago, Isaiah the Prophet wrote the words that poured over my soul like a balm. What an unexpected blessing!

A new friend gave me a book to read about comfort in the wilderness that is described in chapter 40 of that Old Testament book. We were traveling in Israel seeing that wilderness at the time.

Dry, rough and desolate comes close to describing the place. My soul could relate!

The trip prompted my two year in depth study of Isaiah. This was a verse by verse study of the scripture. Each class member was encouraged to read and write each word of the passage assigned for each day. We were all learning to allow the Holy Spirit to be our teacher. I am sure that this exercise in obedience was a major part of what held me together.

In John 1:14 we are told: "The Word became flesh and took up residence among us." Jesus Christ is like super glue working His way into your soul and holding all things together. (Colossians 1:17)

His Word kept me from falling apart. I am not sure how. Many times my mind could only comprehend a few words. I was a miner digging for anything to give me hope.

I also thank God for the prayers of our loved ones and few friends that knew some of what was going on. I had begun to share my pain with a few close friends. No one had any answers, just prayers.

I say that not in a condescending tone, just one that is facing reality. The lack of understanding of most of our friends, as well as the shame of our son's choices, led us more and more into isolation.

The drug addiction cycle produces a life of its own that at the final stages makes the addict unable to choose healing. After years of seeking council, we learned that many well-meaning advisors offer weak humanistic answers. Basing a drug recovery program or a counseling session on the premise that human beings are inherently good will never produce true healing.

We cry out alone.

As I write this, I wonder how Michael Jackson's mother must have felt. She surely was surrounded by a great host of people upon the death of her son. How did she cope in her brokenness?

Maybe the number of visitors is not the key.

For me,

No one brought food or flowers;

No one held my hand or prayed with me in the waiting room.

No one visited this mother of a drug addict.

Chapter 2
Our Andrew

Louis and I were married in college and the year I graduated we had our first sweet baby. Olivia came in to my life when I was alone in a new town with few friends. Louis had his new engineering job and I had a new baby. The next year we were blessed with our dear Melissa. Needless to say with two babies, 13 months apart, our lives were full of all the things new families enjoy: lots of laughter, singing, yelling and crying, plus a lot of cooking and cleaning up!

I was able to stay home with the girls for several years. I enjoyed this special time of playing, gardening, and visiting our friendly neighbors. The yard had flowers in bloom all three seasons, and a good sized vegetable garden. Our family seemed complete and I did not ever think we would have any more children. Having twins the hard way filled my plate. I began working part time when the girls were about three and four. Louis had taken a great job offer and we moved to a larger town where there was a greater need for designers.

After I had started my own design business, when the girls were 10 and 11.....and I was moving forward with my professional dreams, we found out we were going to have a son. Wow, I was mixed with all the emotions of pregnancy. I was not sure I was up to another baby to rear. We were super busy.

The girls were in many of the church activities, as well as ballet and piano, Indian princess, and of course school. How would I manage? Louis was super happy to have a son coming. He had a good job that also gave him time to enjoy the family. It took me a few months before the excitement of a new baby began to sink in. I was still not sure how I would manage it all. Andrew's arrival was three weeks later that his due date. I was not a happy camper. He weighed almost nine pounds. Our girls loved having a baby to hold and bounce around. They were a big help and I soon adjusted to the new normal. As an infant, he stayed at the design office with me for quite a while.

Our family continued in the same pattern we had started our lives together: seeking God's best and working hard to accomplish the American Dream.

We said our prayers when we tucked in the kids and provided as many opportunities for their education and growth that we could afford.

The Bible has always been our guide to Truth. With all the wonderful blessings of following God, I think I must have framed my faith around this premise: "Our good choices bring God's blessing and spares us of disasters." For sure, we all have struggles and make mistakes that cause us trouble. But God spares those that follow Him from the horrors other families face. Right?

The "We know that all things work together for the good of those who love God: those who are called according to His purpose" verse in Romans 8:28 does say that. But so many times we believe God means the good **we** want. This hurricane of events in our family began to teach us differently.

One Sunday our pastor reminded me that a few lines down from verse 28, Paul tells us what kind of "good" he is talking about. Of course it is not the good we would wish for in a fairy tale based life. It is not all comfortable and warm fuzzies good. It is not finding a prince charming or gold at the end of the rainbow. No, it is not necessarily health and prosperity. It is not always easy and positive. The good is explained as becoming conformed to the likeness of Jesus Christ. Much like a potter forming a lovely bowl out of clay. It requires some molding and shaping. Definitely not comfortable. I would not call the life of Jesus, rich, easy or comfortable.

It is no secret our family could use some improvement. God heard our heart's desire to honor and please Him. Now I see that this storm was sent to accomplish our good and His Glory.

Andrew was such a great little guy. Right away we knew he had quite an ability to make friends and lead them to do what he wanted. He was loving and smart. He liked most sports and I was so happy Louis coached some of the teams on which he participated. He especially liked football. His understanding of the game surprised me. He liked designing the plays for his team by drawing and reworking the plays over and over like a coach. All during the games, he encouraged his teammates.

Andrew was a happy child. He was loved and taught so many wonderful things. He was gifted in music and art. Hanging out in a design showroom must have rubbed off. The only real issue he had was three mothers. His older sisters liked telling him what to do and playing rough house with him.

He did survive.

When he was eight, we moved to Atlanta. Many things changed in our family during that time. His sisters had gone to college right before we moved. All of our extended family was in North Carolina. The move was harder than I ever expected. Louis had his new job and I had to close out my North Carolina design business.

I was not doing well. We had moved our home two times in 18 months. I had brought my business home a few months before Louis got the job offer in Atlanta. Three moves in such a short time, all the while our girls were starting college. My business was in debt and that kind of pressure was a real trigger for me. We left all the friends and support system we had developed for 16 years.

A heavy depression settled into my soul. I think it was the first time I had stopped long enough to clearly see my worn out condition, not only physically but in every other way. Exhaustion and depression can cloud our minds to the degree that the quiet voice of Truth cannot be heard. We go into the fear mode of fight or flight. I chose flight. My mind was filled with how to run away.

Where would I go? To whom would I run?

Andrew was the main reason I stayed.

My husband had told me quite clearly, "that if you choose to leave, you go alone."

So instead, we moved! We all ran away. Or maybe, God provided an escape?

The majority of my life challenges have come from the consequences of my loved ones' poor choices, but this was all mine. I could not blame anyone else even though I tried.

The Super Mom I tried to be came crumbling down. For the first time in my life, I could not fake anything. I was faced with my wretchedness. My honesty was brutal. Our Father in heaven knew that I needed a great deal of healing.

Andrew's storm revealed our family problems. Each member is affected by the others. Healing is needed for the entire family. I have no idea how all of my issues played a role in all our children's choices. There is plenty of blame to go around.

This was the beginning of the end of my "fake it 'til you make it" philosophy. As a people pleaser by gift and by training, I had perfected the art. It has come in quite handy in my line of work. No one likes a blunt designer or salesperson. Saying things the "acceptable way" at the "proper time" and with the utmost care not to offend became my specialty.

Lying to myself is probably the worst thing I had mastered. My belief was that most people must be this unhappy. Doesn't everyone fake it?

Self-deception led to a deadened heart that could not determine what I really cared about or believed. Most of my loved ones had ways of strongly promoting their opinions and I avoid conflict, so it was always easier to just cave. I kept my disagreements to myself, not wanting to cause any trouble.

The house that Andrew came home to in those days must have felt like a war zone. Whether I was verbal or silently sulking, the vibes were negative for sure.

Finally, I realized I needed a new heart.

The great thing about having the habit of seeking God is that when you get desperate you go back to what you know. A Bible study of King David was the beginning of the healing I so needed. I was so excited to understand from David's poetry just how honest he was, especially to God. **Somehow, I thought God could not handle my honesty.** That was so freeing to learn. He knew my lies anyway, so why not tell Him.

The Truth will set you free!

During all this time, Andrew was playing baseball and football and enjoying school. He made his profession of faith in Jesus Christ. He was baptized and participated in Sunday school and Royal Ambassador Mission studies. He had a tender heart and cared about his friends. He would invite them to church and I knew the Lord had begun a work in him.

My depression and desire to run away decreased with some rest, Bible study and quiet times. I was not involved in so many activities. I began to read and write in my journals the cries of my heart.

Before I could get very far, a different storm blew up in our home. This time the girls came back home to live. They had made some very poor choices in college and their whirlwind was catching up with them. There were days I did not even get to talk with Andrew about his day. The daily drama and neediness of the girls consumed my time and energy. Time spent fighting insurance companies to pay for care and therapy, as well as finding the proper care was extensive. These issues led me to begin my research on healing of mind, soul and spirit. So many books I studied to help the girls, were meant for me. God has had me in this "breaking the chains" training for quite some time. Each new event opened my heart a bit more to see the changes I needed to make.

Over the next few years Andrew chose to try alcohol and drugs at friends' homes. Many of his friends had these temptations open and available in their homes. We never thought about locking up our prescriptions or the rum bought on a trip to Jamaica. I never even imagined he would drink it.

We did begin to notice an attitude change. Sullen and angry expressions showed up more often. School work was neglected sometimes. We just thought the hormones were kicking in. Then, his music interest changed to what I called screaming music. He started a band called "A Crying Shame" and he did most of the work. He led the promotion, set up the venues, designed the logo and wrote some music. I was at least glad to see him so involved in the music. We figured we were just too old to understand the screaming part.

I can't believe we were so naive.

The signs of the addiction began to show up little by little. The school called about his drinking at a ball game. The counselor recommended a program for parents of kids who were playing with substance abuse. The police were involved in a few incidents. Step by step I was seeing Andrew disappear. His friends changed and he no longer wanted to go to youth group, much less bring his friends. Everything became a battle.

His eyes were always a real sign for me. I could see it when no one else could. That lost look......His pupils might be dilated or his speech slightly slurred. He excused his manic behavior on his self-diagnosed ADHD. We were warned by a couple of friends who had been in this same struggle, that if you suspect a problem, it is much worse than you think.

By driving age, if our kids do not decide to make the right choices for their own good, we have little control. The poison is too available if they are looking for it.

How could my charming, sweet young man decide to play around with his future? Oh... how much I have blamed myself. Then, I would shift to some other family member.

The problems and dysfunction of our family played a part, but ultimately, **Our Andrew chose** to keep on using alcohol and drugs.

Chapter 3
The Truth shall set you Free

How could this happen to us? After all, we are a wonderful Christian family. You know, basically good folks.

There is an invisible visitor that loves to answer that question. He whispers to me at my lowest times, reminding me of all the mistakes and insanities in my life.

There is no telling when the issues began in our family history. Both of our families are filled with dysfunctional members. Therefore, judging your own mental state becomes truly relative.

In comparison to the lives around us, Louis and I seemed pretty normal. We did many of the right things with motives generally bent toward pleasing God. Bible training had been a big part of our youth. We both were leaders in our youth groups and participated in a great deal of church-related activities.

We blended our efforts toward reaching the American dream and trying to follow Christ. It never occurred to us that these goals were not necessarily compatible. We worked hard, served in our church, loved our kids, went on mission trips, sang in the choir, and joined civic clubs. We bought homes and cars. Our tithes were paid, savings for retirement funded and we gave our children as many advantages as we could afford including: ballet, sports, choirs, piano lessons, youth mission trips, and more.

Our calendars were full.

Our credit cards maxed.

Our dreams were coming true.

Slowly, we were climbing the ladder of success afforded by our college degrees. We were taught that if you work hard, make good choices, and get a good education, you could go far in the U.S.A.

As an interior designer, the appeal of beautiful things eventually worked into my soul. I lived with one foot in my world and one foot in the world of the upper class. I would think I was satisfied with my average house, but I never was.

My profession requires an ability to design for them while living in a different tax bracket. The American dream influence was so real that I had the audacity to open my own design firm.

At the time, the decision seemed perfectly normal. I believed this could be the only way to grow my potential. Of course, I would do it much better than those for whom I had worked. I had no experience running a business and very little money to back such an endeavor.

Now I see the insanity.

There were other clues.

Families have secrets. They weave themselves into the fabric of our lives without our knowing it. Very early in my life, I came to understand that my parents grew up very differently than we did. The "country" as we called it had a unique culture. People worked hard and long hours. The children were a part of the labor force on the farm. Each had chores and school work to get done. Enjoying their parent's undivided attention was rare. They grew up under the cloud of the Great Depression on small farms in North Carolina. Everyone would eventually know your troubles. Family problems were cause for shame for the entire family.

Many of my parents' wonderful qualities came through that struggle. Their work ethic, their thriftiness, their Godly attitudes of humility and service created a wonderful foundation for me. That generation was driven to make life better for their children. My parents were no exception.

As I grew up I realized that there were many other issues from their past that affected our family. Out of five uncles and two grandfathers, four were alcoholics. Some were functioning in their struggle and others were destroyed by it.

Out of seven aunts, two had schizophrenia, two obsessive compulsive disorder, one alcoholic and two that had "nerve problems." Or what the general physicians called a woman's inability to control her emotions that resulted in physical problems.

If there is a genetic disposition to any of these problems, we have it. And there never seemed to be any healing, just coping and medications. Few good outcomes happened that would foster hope.

Mental illness declared a life sentence for the entire family.

Some traumatic things happened in my mom's family that no one would speak about. I have only been given glimpses of these events during the episodes that my mother began to have in my teens.

Mother easily got upset when a crisis occurred. Certain things were real button pushers. She had a great desire for fairness and equality. Always keeping an account of how much was spent on many things so that not one would get slighted. She made sure we always knew we were loved and had quality time with her.

Our home was kept clean and decorated even in the most frugal times. Our meals were well balanced, on time and tasty. Dad worked diligently as a life insurance salesman, but came home during his 12 hour day between appointments. His fun sense of humor has saved the day so many times. He could always find a way to help Mom see the humor in things. We were in church "every time the door was open!" Our Sunday nights were the most fun at our house. We would gather around the piano, talking, laughing and singing with friends after church. My sister played the piano, I sang, and everyone joined in whenever they liked. Sometimes guys from our church brought their guitars and added to the fun. Dad's talent was recording it all on the reel to reel. There were so many good times in our home.

And yet, there was something unspoken. A pain that never was discussed but spilled out of Mom's heart at those troubling times. Depression and worry would descend over our house just any ole time. I learned to sense it very early in my life. I would come home from school and know if it was a good day or a "lie low" day.

Some of the events mentioned by Mom included: their house burned down and she hid in the fields, a brother was accused of murder, a crippled sister who was bullied at school, working in the cotton fields with a mean alcoholic older brother that bossed her around, an accusation of betrayal for telling the police where her brother was, and many more. Any small thing could trigger an episode. These long-time covered wounds were opened up each time a family member repeated a similar painful choice. Understanding ways to find healing from her many buried hurts was not even discussed. She was afraid of therapy of any kind. Drugs were never an option for fear of addiction.

Walking on eggshells became my survival skill.

No need to add to her distress. I would just keep it all inside.

My husband's family issues are too similar to believe. The heritage for "crazy" in my children's genetics is unmistakable.

I warned them all about our family history. I told them repeatedly that we could not risk playing around with anything that is addictive. They were told the stories and saw the consequences in each relative's life.

They did not heed the warning.

Each one chose the boundaries they would cross. I am sure they believed like most youth that they were invincible. Evidently, they did not see the horror that I did growing up. It was just stories to them.

One of the saddest consequences of those choices was their need to come back home and bring their trouble with them. Again, the entire family was affected. This kept us in the compensating for one another and recovery mode. It felt like we kept taking four steps forward and ten steps back. Sometimes in my head, I could hear James Taylor singing his song "Knocking around the Zoo," about living in a mental institution. Does anyone else live this way? What will happen next?

My addictions were not obvious. My ability to adapt and compensate worked well for me for quite some time.

To avoid conflict, I developed a great skill for lying. Oh, they were not harmful, malicious lies, just ones that kept things peaceful.

I would do anything to keep the peace. Also, I could not let anyone know my flaws. Pleasing everyone placed enough pressure on me as it was. Conflict would send me to my room in a heartbeat. Correction would make me cry. My heart was tender and in need of a great deal of affirmation. I worked hard to get it. I learned how to use my emotions to get out of trouble. This pattern continued on into my married life.

But Lying is a SIN. For me it was a slow killer like eating too much sugar. I know, because eating sweets was my favorite physical addiction.

After so many years of playing these games, I lost myself.

What was worth arguing over? Since my opinion was not accepted, then it must be worthless, so I became compliant and quiet.

Again, the answers came to me from God's Word. Its pages are filled with brokenness. Every imaginable dysfunction is described in the lives of His children.

Where did I lose sight of this truth?

The first chapter of Isaiah says that God understands about rebellious children. **All** of His children are filled with it. It was not His intention.

Our ancestors chose it and so do we.

It has come to my attention that we can understand that **we** are sinners, but surely not our children. Bless their hearts! Our precious little ones are just having a bad day. Or they were mistreated by a wicked teacher. Or they must not have heard what we said; excuses, excuses.

We either make acceptable sinful choices or we make unacceptable sinful choices. It does not matter, the wages are the same. The consequences are a little different. It is like choosing your poison: eating lots of sugar or shooting up some cocaine. They both kill.

One is a slow subtle killer, the other is quickly lethal.

The same is true for our children. Each step of their maturity gives them more and more opportunity to choose obedience or rebellion.

Rebellion is more fun. At least in the short run, right?!

My understanding of this truth transformed my praying for my family and loved ones. God gave me Ephesians 1:16-19 as a prayer. He can open the eyes of their hearts to know His power in their lives. When they stop listening to us, we pray they hear from Him.

The verse in Romans 3:23 "For All have sinned and fall short of the Glory of God" means **all**. Without the intervention of God's great love, we are **all** in need of forgiveness and healing.

His Spirit living within us and our obedience to Him brings victory over these shortcomings. Our kids are accountable for their own choices, thankfully it is not ALL my fault!

You see my sins were acceptable. That is, the few that I ever admitted to.

Editing the truth to meet the need of the moment left me passionless. I was numb to most everything and felt little motivation. I did not really know what I believed or cared about. My heart felt like a stone. In my despair, I asked God for a new heart. The old one was hardened and worn out. As I mentioned earlier, the study of the life of King David brought me hope. His honesty with God was so refreshing. Layer by layer, God has been revealing the areas of pain and insanity in my life.

I adhere to this definition of insanity; "Choosing to do the same thing over and over expecting different results." At some point, if you want to heal, you must stop and try something new. So, I began to tell myself the truth.

Telling others even took more courage and healing.

Deciding exactly what you believe is critical. There has to be something solid and grounded in which to place our faith. Comparing myself to others did not bring an honest evaluation. I may appear together; all the while I am falling apart on the inside.

Thankfully all those years of singing "On Christ the Solid Rock I Stand, all other ground is sinking sand" paid off. Just the simple act of believing that **God truly loves me**, no matter what was going on, opened my life to His healing.

My own healing and forgiveness from God, has been crucial to my ability to forgive Andrew. Seeing myself as sick as he was, leveled the ground at the foot of the Cross of Christ. We place our "sins" in levels of shame, but God calls it all simply sin. We miss the mark no matter how good we seem. I need to daily remember that God's grace and love are needed equally by everyone.

Having a son that is a drug addict does not feel like God's love. The ground did not feel solid most of the time. My **feelings** had to give way to my **faith**.

His truth shall set us free.

Chapter 4
Put the Baby in the Basket

Our children are always our children. When I was younger, I thought you had them for 21 years and then they went their way. In this generation, they may leave intending to stay gone, but the door to our home has been a revolving one. We allowed them to come back. Each one came back several times.

My parents believed, "You make your bed hard, you lie in it." I grew up knowing there was a time to take responsibility for myself. Plus, I did not ever see myself living with them. Even the summer break in college was difficult to be placed under their rules. Adult responsibility began in our twenties. Thankfully I married a hardworking educated guy. He was taught the same responsible attitude that I was. Even the idea of going back home for me was a real incentive to work at my marriage. Our lives were blessed by making good choices based on our understanding of all we had been taught.

Not so with my kids. Each one started out doing great. Adorable children that were smart, sweet and obedient. The normal growing pains and sibling arguments were expected. Each one has their own gifts and talents. They are each very different people. Olivia excelled in dance, English and social skills. Melissa excelled in piano, math and science.

Andrew excelled in leadership, art and of course, whatever he wanted. We were pleased they each chose to attend college. Each one had their issues, but we felt their choices would improve with a little growing up. I was not happy with all their friends or some of the activities of their teens. After age 16, parents have very little control or influence. We thought we had given them the foundation that would carry them through their youthful stupidity. The enemy had other ideas.

He has tried to destroy all three of them.

We have cried and prayed.

We gave them many chances to try again. At the time we also had the funds to fix some of the messes they made. Sometimes we could not.

I never wanted to stop being supportive. Even with our continued reminders of how one poor choice can change your life, they chose to do their own thing. When a grandchild entered the family, our concern for this little one became a major factor in our decisions.

Ok, I know about the term "enabler." I understand the problem of codependency. But when you are in the middle of all the craziness, you just can't see it. You feel so overwhelmed you can't think. Sometimes the chaos was on all fronts. Usually with only a day or two break between each crisis.

Knowing when to help, intervene, or when to let go is very heart wrenching. They are my children. I love them and will do anything to help them. They know that. But sometimes God has to teach parents a very hard lesson.

My children are not ME.

I am not them.

They have other resources.

And I have a life to live.

I did not figure that out on my own. At a point of being totally overwhelmed with the needs of my kids, I sought a psychologist to help me cope. She was a great listener. She also asked some questions that I had never thought to ask. A turning point came for me when she asked, "Has anyone ever told you that your children have other resources?"

How did I get that so wrong? I believed it is all on us as parents. I have now learned my pride was intertwined with their success. Rarely do we want to admit there are difficult issues that our family member needs to overcome. Have you ever seen a post on social media from a mother sharing the need for her child to find the best mental hospital? Not likely.

There is a certain idolatry that can creep into our hearts in regard to our kids. We invest so much into them. Our hearts get tied to them as we spend so much of our lives loving and teaching them. We need them to do well to validate our efforts. When they didn't I felt so much like a failure. The enemy taunted me with the what-ifs and if-only of all our mistakes... especially when **all** three children make poor choices.

The other issue that I have learned plays a big role in the family is the understanding of respect and accountability.

Because I believed I was responsible, my kids did not have to be. Holding your kids accountable requires a great deal of energy. It brings maturity much sooner. Requiring respect for the rules of the house seemed to work with our kids until about age 16. Then the freedom they acquired at that age gave them the opportunity to display the truth of their hearts.

Resting at night is one of my basic needs and favorite times. After you have your babies, it is never a sure thing. When they are under the same roof they live and sleep in the haven of home. My trust in God's protection was tested when they were not there or in situations that I was not overseeing.

I adapted to them being out and about during late evenings in their late teens. I would pray for their protection and go to sleep. If they were later than expected the fear would cause me to pray a bit more. But when their choices were placing them in harm's way, I needed help.

The Lord taught me this Bible story in a different way:
You remember Moses.
I remember **his mother.**
Can you imagine expecting a baby boy during an edict from the rulers that all baby boys would be killed? Can you imagine the what-ifs in her life? The fear must have

overwhelmed her especially being pregnant. The day came and she delivered a beautiful baby boy.

OH MY! What a joy! What a sorrow!

She could hide him for a while. Maybe the law would change. Maybe no one would hear the cries. But, she had seen the other babies thrown into the river.

These mothers were not spared. How could she believe she would be?

I am sure she prayed for a miracle. It did not come.

The child could not be quieted for much longer. So she decided to let him go. Sometimes it is the only way.

She prepared a basket. Lined it with blankets and tarred it to keep out the water. She placed her dear sweet Moses into the River of Death. The very one into which the boy babies had been thrown. Only God could spare her son.

She had to reckon him dead to her. He was not her son, he belonged to God. She could not save him. If he was spared, it would be His choice

So that began many years of me putting the baby in the basket. I would go through the physical motions as if I was Moses' mom. I would place my loved one that was in harm's way in the River of Death knowing without God's intervention they were lost or dead. It was my way of letting them go. But this was not done blindly.

Our Heavenly Father is the "other" resource that can always be available to our family. It was my decision to leave them in the Father's care.

As I closed my eyes, I asked God to intervene and watch over them. I was then able to slowly go to sleep. During the daytime, I would, of course, take back the role of solving whatever issue came up. At least I could sleep. Step by step the basket exercise was teaching me to trust in God's abiding care for those I place in HIS basket.

Chapter 5
Is this My Son?

Each time Andrew would go to the hospital, he would return home with no options for rehab. His despair was growing and his drug use began to spiral out of control. It always amazed me how he managed to get more drugs, hide it more places, manipulate us in ever more inventive ways.

Andrew used his God-given sales skills to convince us that the methadone clinic in Cartersville, GA was his best choice for recovery. Of course in our ignorance we were open to try anything that was legal. He led us to believe that taking methadone was the best way to get off of drugs safely when there was no medical rehab available. As you can see, we wanted to believe him. Our clarity and judgment were highly affected by the constant hurricane in our home.

We needed help.

By this time, Andrew had been in many classes, several hospital detox wards, two drug treatment programs, and a halfway house.

In his heart, he really wanted to be free of his addiction. Each time he tried and failed, his hope lessened. Sobriety lasted about six months after the first program, and over a year after the short-term Christian program.

In the middle of all this effort at recovery, Andrew and his girlfriend from high school had a sweet baby son. During the one year sobriety, they decided to get married: that is a lot of stress to be subjected to during a time of recovery.

In the end, he could not sustain either relationship. Before they had been married a year, his wife left him, and he returned to drugs. I am not sure which came first, but this return was different; the drugs grabbed hold of him with a vengeance. The brokenness of his marriage clouded any hope that he had of getting it all together.

His mother in law took care of the baby in her childcare before the breakup but now she had him a great deal of the time. When Andrew had him on weekends, he brought him to us. He wanted to take care of this cute little one, but realized he was not able.

This was the time of the loss of his job and halfway house eviction. The first chapter of this book relates this part of the story.

He was living with us; we really wanted to help. He is our dear son, our only son. He is the baby of the family, and we loved him in spite of the craziness he was causing. It was clear to us now that Andrew was a substance-controlled young man we did not know, and could not fix.

Nevertheless, we kept trying.

One Saturday, Louis and I decided to get a better understanding of this methadone treatment. Our suspicion that this was just a legal substitute for heroin was verified in our research. We wanted to know what the clinic's plan to lower the dosage to get Andrew drug free. We both went to speak with the doctors about the plan.

Going into the clinic gave us plenty of evidence to see this was a way to control a problem, not solve it. The long time addicts who have run out of options stand in line to receive a week's supply to carry them until they come back. Their faces are filled with despair and sadness, a picture that tore my heart apart.

"NO HOPE" was the shout coming from the silence.

This eye-opener was just what we needed. The doctor explained that he did not think this was the right program for Andrew because of his age and potential. Now that it was clear to us that this was not the direction to go, we had an intense talk with Andrew. He decided not to come home with us. Our conversation was about how we could not support this treatment anymore. Of course we would have to find another way. Andrew was 20 years old and able to make this decision. We decided to go home, expecting to get a call to come and get him later that day.

Halfway home, we did get a call, but to our horror it was the police. Andrew took a double dose of his Methadone and was barely able to stand up. He would not go with the medics in the ambulance.

Our hearts pounded to get back there in time.

Authorities cannot help you if you refuse their help. He was in the clinic parking lot, surrounded by medics and policemen who were making every effort to get him some help. We coerced him into our car and the medics told me to pound on his chest to keep him awake and alive.

The short trip to the emergency room in Cartersville, Georgia, escorted by police cars and an ambulance was excruciatingly long. I yelled and pounded until we could get him inside the doors of the hospital. The medics followed behind us but could do nothing until he was inside. The hospital staff took him out of our grasp and began all efforts to save his life. We sat in the hallway right outside his room and listened as the male nurse kept him awake until the counter drug took effect.

Every cell in my body was praying for God to save him. Every thought was that His answer might be NO this time.

No matter what you believe or how much faith you have in God, at those times the heart of a mother is desperate.

You would think by this time I would have been accustomed to these incidents. In some ways I was a bit numb, but when faced with the death of your child;

All practice proves useless.

The attending nurse came out after spending a great deal of time keeping Andrew awake. He was loud and strong and I was so thankful for him. He said Andrew was hanging in there and we would just have to wait and see. Louis had a business appointment to keep. Because our business was so fragile and each sale a must, I had no energy to oppose his leaving. I wanted to get angry but I had lost any reason. Life cannot stop every time this happens. Or should it? Anyway, I was glad for the quiet. I did not even think to call someone for prayer.

I went for a walk down the hall and found a chapel.

Quiet and alone, I could not pray. How much more could we go through? Was this our new normal?

The faces of the hopeless methadone addicts crowded my mind.

Was that the future for Andrew? NO, it would not be!

I saw a book on the front altar and decided to go read it. It was a prayer request book written in by other visitors.

With a resolute mind, I wrote my request:

"Father, if you are not going to totally heal and use my dear son, Please take him home.

He is your son. I give him totally to you."

How long it had taken for me to get to this decision! The chains fell. Peace flooded my heart. I would not carry the load any longer. Not during the daytime or nighttime.

So I went to get a bite to eat. I texted a friend and asked for prayer. She is so dear and I was so daft. I did not tell her we were in Cartersville, not Marietta. She went to the local hospital looking for us.

She called and said "Nancy, are you ok?

Where are you?"

Oh my, Praise God, someone tried to visit!

Childhood photos of Andrew

Football and Baseball photos and His Dad assisting in His Baptism

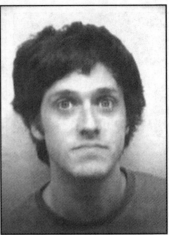

Teenage changes, entrance into rehab photo,
and playing with his son

Andrew and his son at Georgia Teen Challenge

Andrew and his son at Atlanta's Winter Jam concert

Andrew Preaching

Revival on the River was started by Andrew and is a part of "Take the City"

Joy of Jesus!!

Andrew with his sister, Olivia, blessing the children of Help 4 Haiti

Chapter 6
Please Send a Big Fish

It is easy to believe a dramatic wake-up call will motivate us to make a change in our life, even if it is short-lived. Not for the addict. Let me repeat: at some point, the chemical addiction takes complete control. The line can be crossed at different levels of drug use by each person. No one knows when playing around with a substance will turn into an addiction. Once the line is crossed, you are not dealing with the same person.

After the methadone overdose, we no longer believed anything Andrew said. His need for drugs became the focus of his days. All the things he was proud he had never done during his earlier relapses, he began to do. Some of my jewelry was missing. A business check disappeared. It required constant effort figuring out the ways he was able to buy the drugs. Strange cars would show up in the cul-de-sac at odd times. He even made a buy at a grocery store while shopping with his dad. Louis turned around and missed him for about five minutes. He returned a bit less agitated.

He was impossible to control without locking him up. He had to be selling to have money to buy.

He was smooth and hard to catch. God's grace helped me disconnect with love. I kept telling God that Andrew was his son, not mine.

One Friday in November 2009, I came home from work and picked up the mail. In a matter of minutes, I knew something had to change. Included in the pile of bills was an envelope from a psychiatrist who had seen Andrew a couple of times. Enclosed was a hand-written note to me along with copies of prescriptions he said he had not written.

His accusation was devastating. I could envision the DEA driving up and arresting Andrew at any moment. It was clear we were not helping him. He looked like death walking.

An intense coldness flooded my heart.

My face became stern, my mind was set more than I had ever known. It was like choosing to let your son fall off a huge cliff. I told him to get his things in his book bag and leave. He could no longer live at our house. We were doing him more harm than good. I watched him walk away knowing he would probably not survive a day, especially in the cold, out on the streets of Atlanta.

Nevertheless, I was as sure as I have ever been about anything.

He left with just a backpack and a puzzled look on his face. Intense fear swept over me.

Was this the last expression I would see?

My dependence on the Word of God was all I had. The practice of seeking solace in the Bible had to produce fruit.

I did what the Bible study teachers tell you not to do. I allowed the Bible to open wherever it would, needing comfort, any comfort, and any hope.

Please, God. You must be kidding... Jonah?

And yet, as I read the story it was written for me.

We were the people in the sinking boat. Our efforts to save him and the boat had failed. All the while, Andrew was silently yelling to throw him overboard before all was lost. He needed saving. He had been running from God. Did I really need to throw him out so we could survive?

I kept reading and God's peace filled my heart. As parents, we were trying to do **God's job**. And then I remembered that he is not my son. I gave him once more to God. Then the still small voice of God asked me, "Do you believe I can send a Big Fish?"

"Yes Father, you are the only one who can save! PLEASE send a Big Fish!"

The following weekend was like living in suspended time. We were going through the motions of living, but fully expected to visit a jail or the morgue. All the while, praying for a call from Andrew. Thankfully, I remembered to tell him to call us when he was ready to get help, even though we had no options for him. Louis and I were exhausted, almost hopeless. Every effort we had made for the last three years had failed. We could not afford a Program or any other option.

If he did call us, what would we say?

Sunday morning we decided to go to church as was our custom. We both taught Sunday school classes. In our numbness, we continued to do what we knew to do.

I felt like hiding out, but staying busy can delay some horrific pain.

We were carrying what Max Lucado called a "Twin Tower crater" in our hearts! Our effort to go on with our lives required some denial of the severity of all that had been occurring. Especially at church we are conditioned to downplay the negative and report only good things. Our hearts were silently praying for a rescue for Andrew.

Some of our friends knew a few of the problems but not nearly the full picture. But that day, it did not matter what anyone thought. Louis told the Sunday school class our heartbreak and fears, that we had not heard from Andrew and needed prayer.

That Sunday was a special day for our church. Our Sanctuary had been remodeled and this was the day to celebrate. My heart was not into all that money spent on buildings, while I just needed to help my son. Because of this event, Louis' class had a visiting couple who had previously attended our church. They heard Louis' request for prayer and the desperate cry from his heart. At the end of the class the gentleman came up to Louis and said the most incredible thing:

"There is Help and Hope and His Name is Jesus.

Have you ever heard of Teen Challenge?"

He then told of his work with Pastor Coffey in Tennessee. This wonderful man is called to rescue the perishing. He spends his time now working with addicts to get them off the street, out of jail and into the right Teen Challenge program.

Louis began to soak in what he heard. After the worship service we got in the car and before we moved, Louis told me what had happened. My heart caught a glimmer of hope.

Would this be what we would do if Andrew called? He had now been in the belly of the Fish two days. Would I ever hear his voice again?

Just call, Please God help him call. We have an option now!

We began to discuss how we would accomplish the plan Pastor Coffey suggested.

Waiting is not my favorite thing. So instead I went to visit a friend in the hospital hoping to get my mind on someone else with life-threatening issues. It really does keep you a bit balanced. Right in the middle of the visit my phone rang!

IT WAS ANDREW.

I took a deep breath and went out into the hall to talk to him. I held my breath as I heard his cry for help. With all the calmness I could muster, I told him we had found some help and if he was ready his dad would come and get him. He said he would call his dad and tell him where he was. Then during the call to Louis, he changed his mind and said he was not quite ready. Now I was flooded with fear and regret.

What if I had messed up so much that he would not come back? I was so cold and firm.

My imagination went wild with fears of what could happen to him. Nothing felt sure. What if he overdosed, or disappeared or lost his phone?? The drug dealers had threatened to beat him up before. Would they do it now? We just had to wait.

I went back to what I know. I placed him in the basket in the river of death like Moses' mom. I remembered it was three days for Jonah in the Big Fish, that Andrew was not mine anymore, and best of all, that God's arm is not too short to save. I finally went to sleep.

The mental fog of Monday morning was abruptly interrupted by the phone.

Andrew did call back.

He asked his Dad to come get him. Louis went downtown.

Andrew was not where he said he would be.

My Lion-hearted husband started looking for him. When Louis found him, he pleaded for Andrew to come. He even waited and watched him finish his drugs before he helped him into the car.

Oh, what love we have for our children. Oh, what love the Father in heaven has for his!

Just like Jonah, it took three days for the Big Fish to spit him up. What a mess!

It was difficult to believe this was the young man who grew up in our house. The light in his eyes was gone. Death hovered over his entire being.

We had a plan. As advised by the pastor, we made no stops except a shower and some food, then straight into the car to Tennessee. We examined his luggage but forgot to check his clothing. Evidently, he hid some pills in his socks to carry him over. Our two hour trip gave us time to explain to Andrew what we were doing.

I do not know what he understood, but he came willingly.

After spending time counseling with Pastor Coffey, Andrew was taken directly for detox in a Tennessee clinic that knows exactly what the Teen Challenge program wanted for Andrew: no psychiatric prescriptions except what was necessary to provide a safe and complete detoxification.

We drove home marveling at the mercy of GOD.

Andrew's help had finally come. Within such a short time he went from living on the streets to beginning an incredible journey. A Teen Challenge in southeast Texas was to become his home, ten miles from the nearest store. There was no place to run to if he decided to leave. Getting him there required one more hurdle.

After the medically supervised detox in Tennessee, we had to take him to Nashville in order to get a nonstop flight to Texas. We had been warned that taking him to Atlanta Airport was still too risky with all his drug contacts here.

The first six weeks after you stop the drugs are one of the most vulnerable times for a recovering addict. Their bodies scream for relief. Most addiction programs do not understand that the fog in their minds can last four-six months. Gaining maturity to enjoy life can take years.

On the trip to Nashville, we could not let him out of our sight. His flight was the next morning and so to secure him during the night, Louis slept at the door to our hotel room. We were not going to let anything stop this miracle if we could help it. All the arrangements were made for him to be picked up by the Teen Challenge folks in Texas.

Once he was on the plane, we could begin to relax. Our job was done. Back into the basket, he went. God could take it from there. Our hope was rising. We knew it was just the beginning of a long recovery but we could see God's hand in it this time. Now we really thought we could enjoy a rest.

We had the trip back to Atlanta to begin to unwind and talk about all the incredible miracles of the past two weeks. It seemed unbelievable and yet so like God to surprise us with His provision, just at the right moment.

Chapter 7
Punching Holes in the Darkness

So all is well, right? Not for Louis and me. There are no 12 month recovery programs for parents to attend. We had work and the normal routines of life to maintain. The problem was that Andrew had made a mess and we were left to deal with it. I am not talking merely about the left-over drug paraphernalia hidden in the ceiling tiles, or the expensive car with hidden drug compartments. I am talking about his relationships.

In the middle of all this was a lovely young wife from whom he was separated, and their precious two year old little boy. He was being cared for primarily by his maternal grandmother.

Andrew had lost his right to be with his son without our supervision for several months. Our time with him had been very limited as well. It was somewhat understandable in light of all we were dealing with. We also did not know all the legal trouble that Andrew had on his plate. The reality of all these things came to light much faster than we could have imagined.

We were not prepared for what happened next.

Before we could settle in for the ride home, Louis' phone rang and we were notified that we would not be able to see our grandson. The lawyer said that the maternal grandparents were petitioning for adoption.

How could that be happening at this very moment? And why could we as grandparents not see him? I was devastated and confused. I almost lost my son and now I am going to lose my grandson?

This was the last straw.

My heart felt like a punching bag that had the stuffing knocked out of it.

Fear was my first response and then ANGER!

I was scared they would win the court battle. My family's experience with legal matters gave me no hope of any outcome but loss. I tried to talk to his grandmother to understand why we could not see him. She told me we did not give him the proper care. That was not the first time she had told me that.

Almost every conversation of ours over the past two years was filled with her requirements of how we should take care of our grandson. Granted, I was not up on all the new vehicle safety seat laws, but not eating peanut butter before a certain age baffled me. Most weekends after he had been in our care, she gave us a "teacher's reprimand" regarding another rule we had not followed.

I have been caring for children since I could help my mom in her daycare. I am 15 years older than this woman. This constant criticism did not help an already stressful relationship. Her choosing to adopt our grandson from our family drew the final battle lines. She was the enemy. Not only did I have the need to recover from years of living with an addict, I was being questioned on my ability to care for children! No one had ever even hinted those kind of fears about me. I was imagining all the past insanities of our lives brought up in court to prove their case. In the depths of my heart I wondered if she could be right. The enemy was having a field day. Maybe no other child should grow up around us. Our record was not very good at this point. That is when hatred and fear came over me with a powerful, heavy darkness.

I needed some light to show me what was really true.

During this storm, I was leading a ladies' Bible study. It tied me to my Anchor. It required me to study the Scripture each week, verse by verse. This was the **light** in my darkness. Isaiah 40 became my life chapter. The theme is comfort in the wilderness. But for **this battle**, I needed a new promise from God. Something I could cling to when the fear and pain would overtake me.

The Bible tells us in many places to "cry out to the Lord," so I did. Loud and long, sobbing cries that drained me of all my strength. He knew the truth about me. He was my judge.

During the study we read 2 Corinthians 10:4-5. The apostle Paul is talking about warfare. I could relate. The warfare is really in our minds. He tells us to take every thought captive to the obedience of Christ. All I could think to do was exchange my fear and anger for promises from God's word. It was a moment by moment task. So each morning I would take a promise and try to let it set my day's thinking. Thinking it though did not help much. I needed something stronger.

The answer that came for me was this promise in Job. After all he had experienced, this is what he knew: "I know that You (God) can do anything and that **no plan of yours can be thwarted!**" Job 42:1

I was not given the hope that we would win. I was given the **fact that God WINS.**

From that day forward as I would drive to work, I would get within a couple of blocks of our grandson's maternal Grandparent's house. At first, I just said the words. When that did not help, I started yelling them at whoever could hear. I shortened it a bit to make it a battle cry.

I would add the name of the one I felt was my enemy and in a fighting tone I yelled:

"NO ONE, Not even you __W.W.W.__ can thwart the Plans of My God!

The code W.W.W. for my enemy meant Wicked Witch of the West. I thought it would conceal her name.

This was my weapon for my most difficult battle yet. The louder I yelled, the more hope filled my heart.

First John 1:5b provided a message of hope that tells us that "God is Light, and there is absolutely no darkness in Him." Only Light can dispel darkness. Some days I grew hoarse with the yelling and crying. I remembered creation was accomplished with God speaking. The sound spoken by God changed things, and I needed things to change.

It was not my words but His.

During this desperate time, whether I was yelling or just softly speaking HIS Words;

HIS light began punching holes in my darkness.

Chapter 8
Just Let go and Soar

While I was struggling, God was doing a mighty work in Andrew. The Teen Challenge program was perfectly suited for him. He hated it, wanted to leave and give up. They worked him so hard. He mowed acres of grass with a push mower for months.

It was Texas, after all. He sweated out all that poison. The first time he came home I could see the change. He had a long way to go, but what a difference a few weeks made. He tells that part of the story much better than I. God got a hold of him and changed him. I could see our Andrew coming back, with a new hope. His coworkers had said that two years were needed to really rid him of his addiction. God provided this after his 13 months needed for graduation, by having him go to work for the Emerging Leaders College in Jesup, GA. This kept him in God's training program for another year.

Each time he visited during those two years we could see him being transformed. Andrew's love of life, gifts of leadership, and his grateful character were being molded by the freedom he found in Christ. His love for his son was so exciting.

The fight to be a part of his son's life gave Andrew a drive to continue. He had all the old legal issues expunged from his record. It was so important for him to prove to all of us that his recovery was real. Our bi-weekly visits gave us a chance to watch this genuine transformation first hand.

The way the Lord intervened in the adoption battle blows me away. Both families were visited by the Court appointed guardian ad litem. I spent weeks preparing the house we had moved into so that our young grandson might recognize his things and remember us. When a child is two years old, nine months is a long time. We were only allowed to see him once (not hold him) in those nine months.

The anticipated day arrived and I was anxious about it all. I was so glad I had asked our daughter and her son to be there to bridge the time lost.

Upon seeing his cousin, he warmed right up to us. We all went to show him his room and toys and they began to play.

His happiness and calmness during the visit was evident to the attorney. He remembered us! We were able to reconnect quickly and the love bond we shared was evident. We believe that her report to the judge turned the tide for the entire battle.

In an adoption case, only those petitioning the court can go into the court room. Talk about lack of control!! We waited outside each time hoping we would not lose our grandson. I do not know what was said, but I know that the judge believed that a child should be able to enjoy the love of his entire family. On one occasion, as I peeked into the courtroom door window, it appeared as if our daughter in law was pleading with her mom about something being discussed. Without knowing anything, I felt helpless again and could only pray for a miracle.

In the end, the maternal grandparents chose to stop the adoption. Andrew was awarded joint custody as soon as he graduated from Teen Challenge. My heart overflows with praise as I remember that day.

God does win!

Again in Isaiah 40, a beautiful picture is painted for those who wait and trust in the Lord. The Lord gave me a visual that has helped me so much. I tried to picture myself standing on the edge of a very high cliff, like an eagle about to fly. I would **wait** for the right wind to come along so I could **soar** off the cliff. My arms opened up widely like wings to accept the up-draft of the wind. My toes grip the edge, I begin to be filled with the fear of falling.

For a bit, the "what-ifs" and "what-now", fill my mind. What could I fix with my arms outstretched?

What could I control?

What might happen with my heart so open and vulnerable? How foolish I must look waiting for that strong wind to take me up. I take a deep breath and listen;

Then the still small voice said,

"Just Let go and Soar!"

Chapter 9
I Stand Amazed

Oh, if I could really live like that, soaring above the craziness of my life. This last year I have been learning that I have one major spiritual work to do: Believe God! It is the only way to enter his rest. I had to stop debating. My preference is to understand and work through issues. You know, figure things out. My problem solving mind can get in the way of accomplishing this simple task. Just Believe!

The other truth that helped me so much is one I learned many years before, but it had to sink into my bones:

Psalm 115:3 states, "Our God is in heaven and does whatever **He** pleases."

This world tells us to view the events of our lives as if it was all about me. The universe must make me comfortable and happy. That core mistake takes us all down the road of despair. We keep getting disappointed. Our Creator is the One with the instructions for our lives.

As a child a favorite chorus of a hymn started like this: "Turn your eyes upon Jesus/look full in his wonderful face/ and the things of earth will grow strangely dim/ in the light of His Glory and GRACE."

It has taken five years to gain a more heavenly perspective of all this pain. Each interwoven event had a purpose, one that is much larger than I could ever see in the midst of the storm.

The legal battle to adopt our grandson away from our family could not ever be considered a "good thing" to me. The Apostle Paul in the New Testament warns us of taking things to court that should be settled within the Family of God. I learned long ago that usually the only winners are the lawyers. It caused a great deal of anguish.

We depleted our final savings on the lawyer fees and traveling expenses for Andrew.

We missed almost a year of our grandson's growing up. If they won, he would not remember us and never have his family name.

Andrew was put in challenging circumstances trying to get to court proceedings in Georgia all the way from Texas. He left the security of Teen Challenge during his vulnerable months three times to be in bus stations and airports where drug use is out in the open.

Stressful too, was the very strained relationship of the Grandparents. It was a time our families needed to support and encourage each other.

Andrew and his wife were real young. We needed to help them become the best parents they could, not be in a court battle.

Who could take that mess and make something good of it?

A **heavenly perspective** comes with time, forgiveness and grace.

Look for it. Ask God to help you see it.

First, the loss of our financial security prepared us to better understand trusting God for every need. This kind of faith is a true requirement in our recently formed ministry to help the orphans in Haiti.

Instead of losing our grandson, we enjoyed his bi-monthly weekend visits with us. Those visits also afforded time to reconnect with our son.

When the miracle of the joint custody decision happened, Andrew moved to a Georgia Teen challenge program to be close to his son, with the full support of his Directors. That move gave him an opportunity to learn about the Emerging Leaders College in Jesup, Ga. After he graduated the initial program, he was asked to work there.

The director for that college is the son of the President and CEO of Teen Challenge, International. Upon witnessing God's great gifting and favor on Andrew's life, he was hired to work for Teen Challenge Southeast in Columbus, Georgia. All of that afforded him the ability to spend every other weekend and holidays with his son.

Each step that looked like happenstance, led to the next provision for Andrew's calling. The complications of this legal battle became the stepping stones for their future.

Our families have learned to pray for one another and work together to care for our dear grandson. Reconciliation started with a meeting for lunch. Just Grandmother to Grandmother. We could start by agreeing about our mutual love for him. We shared some stories and some laughs. I learned that the rift had become obvious to our grandson, so that made it imperative for me to reconcile. She knew her W.W.W. name. Oh, my!

I had tried to find forgiveness toward their family. Focusing on this heavenly perspective allowed me to see God's overriding control in this situation, making forgiveness much easier.

I Stand Amazed.

Chapter 10
Happy Dance

The last three years have afforded our family many reasons to celebrate. My husband loves to celebrate. I came from a family that had small quiet celebrations. Not so with the Chalmers family. So I have learned, when you get the chance, you DANCE.

My dear friend, the only person to try and visit me during this entire ordeal, told me it was surely time for a Happy Dance. So when Andrew and his son were to stand in front of 20 thousand young people at an Atlanta Winter Jam Concert, I invited my friend to come with me. I knew she would join me in the happy dance. As he gave his testimony and invited the crowd to find freedom in a new relationship with Jesus Christ, my heart soared above the earth-bound things.

The miracles just keep happening.

Over the last three years, Andrew has launched a new ministry called **Take the City**. Step by step they are bringing hope to an entire region in Georgia. The Chattahoochee Valley area is just the beginning for **Take the City**. God has allowed our son to travel many places around the world sharing his story of hope.

Countless people have been led to know the Christ who rescued and changed his life.

I visited the group that has joined Andrew in this ministry as they met in his home. These young people have a heart for sincere worship and changing their world. They were getting ready for their second "Revival on the River" in the spring. God worked in mighty ways last year as my husband and I witnessed. Sitting in the crowd, and watching over 3000 people from the Chattahoochee Valley area enjoy the worship, afforded another big happy dance. There have been many others.

Andrew has a desire to minister wherever he goes. It can be quite comical at times. We might be going on a family trip and stop for coffee. Our aim is to do this quickly and keep moving.

We all look around and ask each other, "Where is Andrew?" He is oblivious to our timeline and we find him in a corner praying and blessing someone in the coffee shop.

Happy Dance again.

The sweetest personal time was a phone call just to me. After a regular conversation, Andrew asked me, "How are YOU, Mom?" then he asked if he could pray just for me. How special for God to use him that way. God has gifted him with incredible faith and the ability to focus on the needs of others. He sensed my need for additional faith and encouragement. What a special time for me, "The Mother of a Drug Addict," who has prayed for her son so often. He prayed for me!

God is so GOOD!

Happy Dance time!

Yet, there is one more miracle.

Andrew has been awarded primary custody of his son, and we are loading his things to go and live with his Dad. It is quite a big change that will take some adapting for them both. In the middle of all this craziness, I never would have dreamed this day would come. My heart is filled with awe for our powerful Father in heaven that cares about every circumstance of our lives.

The Firm foundation that God gave Andrew while at Teen Challenge developed his leadership ability and his calling. He and his new wife are now leading the **Take the City Ministry** full time. This ministry is focusing on uniting the Body of Christ, mobilizing them through teaching and hands-on experience. It is a powerful way to revitalize our cities using personal outreach and evangelism.

If you would like to read Andrew's testimony go to: http://andrewchalmers.wordpress.com

Father in Heaven be praised!

Chapter 11
Reality Check

It saddens me to say how I still struggle with unbelief. The smallest set back or delay and I come to a crisis of faith. After all I have witnessed......after all the Glory of God revealed to me.....after all the joy of seeing miracle after miracle.....

My daily choice is to TRUST and OBEY.

Our family has been given a second, third and fourth opportunity to grow in His love. God's grace just pours out from the heart of His dear Son. We are precious in His sight. WOW!

The times He held me in the Emergency Room, steadied my soul to get through another day, encouraged me with a phone call or hug, and reminded me of His truth no matter what things looked like, are so precious to me.

God's special encouragement came to me in another unusual way. Let me explain.

During the same time that Andrew was in Texas starting his recovery, Haiti was hit by a devastating earthquake. This already impoverished nation was now crumbling and more than 200 thousand people lost their lives. Many children became orphans.

Louis had spent previous years helping the victims of Hurricane Katrina in the Gulf coast of the U.S. Now he was watching another crisis on the news, and his heart was compelled to go and help. I was still in recovery mode myself and could not even consider exposing myself to that disaster.

My own need for healing was too great to go and minister to others. Even though I was trying to minister to the ladies in my Bible studies, my motives were primarily my survival.

Nevertheless, God had a plan. All the fear of failure as a mother that I faced over the last years with my children, as well as the battle for our grandson was about to be quieted.

Louis came back with a calling he could not shake.

The needs were so great.

His heart was connected to the Pastor he met while there. The Haitian government had asked this pastor of seventeen churches and three schools to provide care for more and more children.

I did not quite get it.

What could we do? We were at a point of very low resources for ourselves. How could we help feed all these children? Haven't we dealt with enough impossible things?

You know, life is filled with impossible. Whether your child is on drugs or has no food or clothes, we all need God to intervene.

So we started Help 4 Haiti, Inc.

It has been over four years since we began this journey. At this time there are 75+ children that God has asked us to help provide food, clean water, and shelter. Add to that education and medical care and you see how impossible it is.

So how does all this quiet my fears?

A friend shared a comforting thought when I explained our unusual call to Haiti: she asked, "If you and Louis were such terrible parents, why would God give you 75+more children to love and support?" Ok, I get it! How comforting to know that my greatest fear was relieved by a calling to help orphans.

We really love the message of the song by Matthew West, "Do Something." The chorus tells us: If not us then who.../ if not now then, when.../ it's time for us to **do something**.

This adventure is a story for another day. But it reminds me of a major component in God's plan for healing.

I need to help others!

I need to get my mind off my own struggle.

Wow, I thought I had trouble. But my children have never been hungry, have yours?

The enemy enjoys keeping us under our circumstances so that he can accomplish his second most important task. His First priority is to keep us from faith in Jesus Christ. After we become a child of God, he wants us to stay so absorbed with "ME" that we are unusable by God. I believe many of our mental health issues stem from that tactic. Personal healing gives us a chance to be a blessing to those around us. Then we hear their stories and know we cannot fix their problems either. So as we minister to them, we learn to trust God with our own problems.

God specializes in the Impossible and has made sure I am confronted with it quite often. Now I understand why. In His patience, He has taught me to enter his rest. It is when most everything in your life is out of control that His power can be revealed. The secret was to learn what is required of me.

An old Hymn told us all long ago to TRUST and Obey. Wholehearted belief in His Love and Power lead me there. Trusting God is accepting the fact that His plans are the best, and then believing that He truly loves me. I love to read Isaiah 43: 1-4 where He calls his children (ME) Precious in His sight! The children in Haiti understand. They sing "Red and yellow, black and white, they are precious in His sight! Jesus loves the little children."

Church folks don't like to talk about unacceptable problems. Oh, we can go on and on about cancer, death, (as long as it is not suicide), divorce, loss of job, sudden illness, surgery, birth defects, all our "small sins" and many more.

But alcohol and substance addiction, family abuse, runaways, other addictions, mental illness, satanic activity, pornography and sexual perversions, rape, murder, and nervous breakdowns are taboo.

NO ONE VISITS THE MOTHER OF A DRUG ADDICT.

There are few Sunday school classes or small group studies that cover these every day issues in our 21st century culture. Parents have no recovery programs or retreats to attend to recover from difficult times. My heart aches for the families of addicts because the one making most of the huge mess goes to rehab for a vacation (of sorts), and the family goes back to school, work and real life.

We send our kids away....... throw money at the problem and expect things to get better without taking the time to seek healing for ourselves and our family. All these issues are family issues with an underlying spiritual battle, especially for Christian families.

I know my family heritage included many who chose to follow Christ. But we live in a world system of lies that so easily work their way into our souls. We are taunted by the enemy. No one is exempt. That fact hit home when I realized several years ago that all of those taboo issues have occurred in our extended family.

The enemy wants us to believe we are alone in our battle and that life will never really get better. He also whispers that no one else would understand or they would judge us. The isolation we endure by believing that lie is excruciating.

If you need reassurance that you are not alone in this struggle, just read the Old Testament. The pages are filled with stories of God's people struggling with the same list.

Without a continual daily surrender to God, we are all one moment away from falling into any of these poor choices.

Our Church families need to open the discussion about unacceptable issues and the pain they cause.

Lord,

Teach us each day to:

Admit our pain and disappointments.

Admit our total inability to reach His Perfection.

Seek forgiveness for ourselves and find healing in His Word.

Get on our knees and Pray LOUDER.

Worship our God with all our hearts.

Open our eyes to His Goodness all around us.

Praise his Greatness, Love and Power!

Chapter 12
Praise and Prayer

Prayer is the best way to open the way for the miracles we need. Simple heart felt conversations, based on our ability to approach the God of the universe because of the sacrifice of Jesus on the cross. Don't give up. Be specific. Ask for someone to agree with you and be your partner. Expect God to accomplish His purpose in the lives of those we love. Build your faith by asking God to direct your search of His Word for the promises He has for you and your loved ones. Diligently study His Word, speak out loud those Promises and watch with hope as God shows up.

The path to wholeness starts with brokenness. I have tried to fix so many things and understand so many things. Letting go of the need to know why... became crucial. Eternity will answer many things that I do not understand. Waiting for His plan is our challenge.

Our physical bodies are called clay pots in the New Testament. When I look into a casket, I truly see that reality. My clay pot is very fragile and has been cracked for quite a while. I believe this process is necessary to grow.

If the process of brokenness is what you are experiencing, be prepared for some type of pain. I really do prefer an easier way for us all. Fortunately, it does not work that way.

Healing is God's specialty since we are His creation. One major delay to finding our healing is that most of us are not sure **we** are the ones who are sick. I can hear Jesus asking,

"Do you want to get well?"

PAIN gets our attention. Do not try to numb it or run from it. Allow God to use it. Look for an inner core issue that needs healing. Open your eyes to understand the purpose of pain and sorrow. Ask God to gently help you work through your pain. Find a Bible based small group study that focuses on real healing. I have added a Reflections study at the end of this book for your own personal use. "Life's Healing Choices" by John Baker is excellent. Quite often, I find the need to remind myself of the principles I learned in that class. As God brings healing to your life, begin to find ways to share your story of hope and comfort to others.

The steps of this journey were painful to walk.

As the Balm of Gilead poured over my heart, my Father in Heaven asked me to share this story.

May each drop of His comfort bring healing and restoration to our families.

All the Glory and Praise belong to Him!

My PRAYER

All praise to you Father in Heaven, for who you are and all you created. Thank You, dear Jesus, for paying the complete sacrificial price for my forgiveness. Holy Spirit, thank you for living in us as teacher and guide.

I ask you, the God of all hope, to bless each one reading this story. May they read your Word and seek you. I am asking for your healing power to pour into all our lives. Strengthen us to focus on what breaks your heart.

Please give us a heavenly perspective on the past. Help us to learn to replace our need to fix people into the joy of loving them. Fill us with thanksgiving for all that you are doing to bring about **Your** plan.

Your Kingdom come!
In Jesus Christ great name! Amen

Nancy Reardon Chalmers
bluegreenwaterinaclaypot

Now we have this treasure in clay jars, so that this extraordinary Power may be from God and not from us.
2 Corinthians 4:7

Notes

Chapter 1   Charles H. Dyer "A Voice in the Wilderness" copyright 2004 Moody Publishers

Chapter 2   Beth Moore, "A Heart Like His" Lifeway Church Resources

Chapter 3   Edward Mote, "The Solid Rock"

Chapter 4   Exodus 2:1-10 Story of Moses Birth

Chapter 5   Pastor Coffey, Anchor Point Ministries, Cleveland, Tennessee

Chapter 6   Max Lucado, joyrenewed.blogspot.com

Chapter 9   Helen H. Lemmel, "Turn Your Eyes Upon Jesus" public domain

Chapter 10   Take the City, Facebook @takethecitycolumbus Andrew Chalmers, founder

Chapter 11   Help 4 Haiti, Inc. Facebook @Help4Haiti Louis Chalmers, founder

Chapter 12   Balm in Gilead, Jeremiah 8:22

About the Author

Nancy Reardon Chalmers grew up in North Carolina in a wonderful family that encouraged love, laughter, music, hard work and trusting God.

She and her husband, Louis (the lion), have been growing together with God's help for over 40 years. They have three children, five grandchildren, and more blessings than they can count.

Her Father in heaven is her best friend. He was with her and held her during this entire storm.

Her mother shared the promise that brought her to faith as a young child when she expressed her first fears.

Jesus said, "I will never leave you nor forsake you"

And He will always be her most welcome Visitor.

Reflections Study guide

Chapter One

Could you relate to the story in the first chapter? Are you ready to share yours with someone you trust?

If so, we need to agree before we begin: what is said in this class stays in this class. Please feel free to include these needs in your private prayers for one another.

Let's face it. We begin to find healing by admitting our faults to one another. Read and write James 5:16.

What is going on in your family?

Who are the players in your drama?

How is all this affecting you?
And your family?

Describe your most recent challenge or storm and how you responded?

To whom do you share this problem, where do you go for good counsel?

How do you find comfort?

Read and study the following verses: (Summarize what they say to you.)
Colossians 1: 15-17

St. John 1: 1-5

Isaiah 40:11

Chapters 2 and 3

When you think back over your life and that of your family..... are there patterns of behavior that were repeated? List a few positive and negative ones.

Which patterns stand out as the most destructive?

Which ones make you smile?

Pray that God will show you at least one issue in your own life. Call a friend and share some stories of childhood or early family events......listen to yourself...Note what you remember that you may have tucked away.

When the pressure is on, which influence from your early years is the loudest? Name the way key family members responded to tough times. Did it help or hurt?

Who needs the most healing in your family?
What are some things you have done to fix the problem?

Read 2 Samuel 12:1-15, what is happening here?

Read all of Psalm 51 out loud. David learned something we must learn. Study it and share the special truth God has for you.

Healing starts with ME!
It is not our responsibility to change anyone else.
Start a prayer list of issues for which you need God's healing.

Chapter 4

Who has the most control in the important areas of your life? How does that work for you?

In what area of your life would you like more control? Why?

What are your greatest fears?

Read Exodus 2: 1-10 think mostly of the Mother and Father of Moses.

There are two other places this story is told in the NT. One is in the Hall of Faith in Hebrews 11:23.

For what attribute did his parents receive recognition in this chapter?

What would you do in this situation?

How much effort do you think they made to save his life?

We all know the plan God had for Moses, but they did not. They could see he was special. When did they finally launch him into the River?

Study and write key phrases from these verses:
Psalm 115:3

Isaiah 43:1-6, 10-23

Isaiah 44: 1-8

Share your understanding of God's Control of all things from these verses.

Are you ready to launch your loved one?

Chapter 5

We have worked on learning some important principles while going through a storm. Take a few moments and review the first 3 weeks. Write the entire verse of Scripture that has helped you the most.

Which part of our study hits home the most and is it a continual problem?

Have your family issues eased at all while you are working on this study?

How often do you want to give up?

Are you settling into the crazy as if it will always be this way?

Read 1 Samuel 1 -2:1-10. The story of Hannah and Elkanah. What was the cause of Hannah's despair?

How did her husband respond to her?

What were the social and economic consequences for a woman with no children?

How did Eli the prophet see Hannah?
What did she finally do? What did it cost her?

Summarize her Prayer of worship.

Is there someone you are holding on to? Why?

What is God asking you to do? How can you record and seal your decision?

Read Hebrews 9:2 and Eph. 1:13
How did God make a vow to us? How was it sealed?

Chapter 6

In a storm we are many times called to make really tough decisions, some are even life or death decisions. The Bible has many stories relating to storms.

The story of Jonah has been a part of my life as long as I can remember. It is easy to group it with many of the fun stories of childhood. Most of those are just myths and fables. But because this tale is in God's Word there is power in this story. Not only does it provide lessons to be learned, like some of the other stories, but it has life giving truth for us to understand.

What Bible story from your childhood do you easily remember?

Was there a character with whom you identified?

Read Jonah chapters 1 and 2, as if this was your first time..

Summarize the story making sure you write the events that stand out to you.

With whom do you identify? Why?
Where was Jonah during this violent wind?
Did Jonah know why the sea was raging?

Why would the other seamen not listen to him and just throw him overboard when he asked them to?

Has God ever called on you to do something that was the opposite of what you would choose?

What was your response?

Does your understanding of who God is encourage your decision to obey or hinder it?

Who are you enabling to go the opposite way from God's call on their life?

What was Jonah sure God would do if he preached in Nineveh?
Jonah 4: 2-3
So why not go?

Where did he end up? Read his prayer again!

Verse 7 -9 says "As my life was fading away, I remembered the Lord... I will fulfill what I have vowed. Salvation is from the Lord."

Memorize Psalm 18:30
Write it here to remember!

Chapter 7

The real world is one of Darkness versus Light. Read Ephesians 5:6-11. We live in a constant warfare while on this earth. The comfort of our American lives numb us to this fact. We want our lives to be easy, instant, and most of all comfortable. The fact that our enemy is not visible creates an illusion that all is fine. His sudden attacks will overwhelm us if we do not stay prepared.

If we do not teach our children the strategy of warfare, **their** issues add another front to our battle.

Who is our enemy and what are his tactics?

Read the following verses and list them.
2 Corinthians 4:4 and 11:14;
John 8:44
Isaiah 14:12-15
1 Peter 5:8,
Ephesians 6:12

When he whispers to you, what is the enemy usually saying? The spoken word is the expression of thought, like Jesus is the Expression of God.

Our enemy uses lies, doubt, and fearful thoughts intended for our destruction as his expressions.

Our spoken words of God's promises release life and activate God's power in the spiritual realm. Remember Moses had to speak to the rock the second time for water to be released. God wanted His people to understand the power of HIS WORDS.

Is everything you think or say TRUE? Your words can bring life or death. Proverb 18:21 Share a lie you believe.

In Ephesians 6:17 what is your only offensive weapon against your enemy?

Who provides the power of your sword?

Read Romans 8:38-39 out loud as often as necessary. Add scriptures you find that fight your particular battle to this list when under attack.

Jesus Christ won The Victory for all time and eternity. The Cross paid for it and the Resurrection sealed it. Claim it!

In Colossians 2:8-15 what was nailed to the cross and who has been disarmed and disgraced? Remind the enemy that you know that truth!

Study the following verses: Psalm 43:4-8;
                Isaiah 59:1-2 and 55:6-11
Write your favorite!

Chapters 8-12

What is your perspective when you are tired, stressed or in the middle of a battle?

Where do you go and what steps do you take to get relief?

Now that we know our enemy, have you developed tactics to battle his insidious whispers of defeat?

List some songs, books or movies that have transported you away from the problems in your life?

What Bible passages do you keep reading for comfort?

Read Isaiah 40: 25-31. Write down the Words God has for you from these verses.

What is required to soar above your circumstances?

Has God shown you some things He is doing through this Storm?

Will you wait, hope, and have faith that He will accomplish His plans in your life?
Look for God's perspective, pray to see it, open your heart to accept His divine plan. Commit a time to get alone to work on these goals.

Happy Dance time is when the smallest thing is accomplished that leads to God accomplishing His will in the lives of our family. Find someone to join you!
Celebrate and savor each one. Fill your heart with Praise that God has a Plan and He will do the work to accomplish it. Philippians 1:6

What is God asking you to do with the Pain, loss and disappointments of your life?

There may be someone that needs a warm hug and a story of God's grace.

There may be someone that has caused you great pain that you need to forgive. As it says in Job 42:10…..and God restored…
….when Job prayed for his friends. After his brokenness, Job showed his forgiveness by praying for his visiting friends.

There are many in great need of your love and comfort in our country and around the world.

Thankfully my loneliness and pain afforded me a wonderful treasure:

No One Visits the Mother of a Drug Addict…except for Jesus!